PRAISE FOR *THE NEAR AND DISTANT WORLD*

"The brilliant poet Bianca Stone moves from strength to strength. Her powerful new book is a deep pleasure, fueled by a necessary restlessness in the service of discovery, creating a gorgeous tapestry of introspection and seemingly endless creative expression. These wonderfully rich and capacious poems explore the 'spectacle of historic grief' set in tension with the 'afterlyric of childhood.' *The Near and Distant World* is bold, daring, darkly funny, heartrending, and honest."

—PETER GIZZI,
author of *Fierce Elegy*

PRAISE FOR BIANCA STONE

"Bianca Stone's poems are powerful, moving, and original."

—SHARON OLDS

"A brilliant transcriber of her generation's emerging pathology and sensibility."

—JOHN ASHBERY

"Bianca Stone is a seeker. Wry, funny, and often thwarted, mired in daily life, metaphysically tormented, afflicted by what she calls 'allergies of the soul,' she searches for something deep and meaningful, something ongoing, mysterious, and ineffable."

—EDWARD HIRSCH

"Bianca Stone's poetry has the glow of 21st-century enlightenment and lyric possession."

—MAJOR JACKSON

THE

NEAR AND DISTANT

WORLD

ALSO BY BIANCA STONE

What Is Otherwise Infinite

The Möbius Strip Club of Grief

Someone Else's Wedding Vows

THE NEAR AND DISTANT WORLD

poems

Bianca Stone

Tin House is an imprint of Zando.
zandoprojects.com

First US Edition 2026
Manufacturing by Kingery Printing Company
Cover and text design by Beth Steidle

Library of Congress Control Number is available.

978-1-963108-65-1 (paperback)
978-1-963108-74-3 (ebook)

10 9 8 7 6 5 4 3 2 1

Manufactured in the United States of America

for Thou

Contents

In the end, in the whole psychology, the self,
The town, the weather, in a casual litter,
Together, said words of the world are the life of the world.

WALLACE STEVENS,
"AN ORDINARY EVENING IN NEW HAVEN"

I

OLD BIO IN SNOW

There's always a snowstorm coming
and I'm always booked at a café
on the other side of the mountain
driving on bald tires to give another lecture
on Hegel's vision
of the infinite whole
and at the last minute deciding to lecture on wind,
and snow, and the effects on discarded newspapers.
No, wait—this lecture
was about repeating the past.

There's always a snowstorm coming
and I'm always booked at a café
on the other side of the mountain
driving in the dark
and I am insanely happy,
weaving along the winding cliffs,
careening down the other side of the summit
in a little blue car, parking, sliding a quarter in a meter
and bouncing off with manila folders under my arm,
my gabardine overcoat
flapping open like a hospital gown,
to give lectures on vision and snow and repeating the past.

And if they introduce me with an old bio
so be it. No need to mention the latest
gummy linguistic situation in words,
or my recent award
for lying on the rug
and staring at the lacy vacant spiderwebs

in the petticoats of a glass cupboard—no,
forget the laurels. What matters tonight is Time
and blizzards
and saving on your next purchase
with a coupon from your unconscious.

Now, snow.
That form of water which haunts.
It follows you indoors in obedience to air
until it feels fire, then it looks for a place to lie down
with fire, to then elope with earth, to move slowly to the sea.

I just thought I knew something
and light was pouring through me onto the floor—
but everything shifts, one moment
to the next, and leaves
a dark stain where it was.

I remember something, then panic sets in.
A metaphor no longer
holds like it used to—I master
no single existence in the past—yet here I am,
still with my name and mutant face.

It's not real they say, the past.
Even if an ember is burning holes clean through,
cherries dropped from the tips of cigarettes, fallen
many years ago—back before they put phones in pockets
and people wrote numbers all over the stairwells
and no one stopped reading a book
to take a picture of one of its pages—ridiculous.
Instead, there were long uninterrupted hours of reading
and smoking and crying. Your own eyes wept

as they do now—though, looking back,
you're not even sure who was weeping and who
was watching the weeping. Time is also about waiting
for an almost imperceptible change
in a single tear. The mother's textured silence.
Disturbed neighborhood kids coming together in the woods
to echo their own households.

It's never really about the *why* in crying, is it? I mean
in terms of narrative
it just comes, resembling meaning
like an old bio, resembling snow, and holding
in your mind the object of a spruce tree
at whose base a kitten is buried wrapped in a tea towel.
And everywhere
there is a white soil coming,
carried sideways by wind, and down by gravity,
a pale inflection on its many cold lips.
And it doesn't need to know where it came from
to know it is part of the whole
and it is snow,
and it falls on your face
and ends.

THEORY

You'll find no theory vengeful enough for this life.
You must keep living it. The greatest revenge
is the unprovable work.
Employed barefoot in the grass, aimless.
But there are times I want
to find not the right psalm
but concept,
to theorize the current
of sadomasochistic reasoning.
But does it unfold me? is always the question.
To be beside it. I have
a tentative pleasure in the academy.
I hover in the indexes, the footnotes.
The vibrant arguments
thrill me. But my greatest fear:
to be condemned to theory.
Without song, without my trash,
my weird ottava rima, my pointless point.

In the night, only the mad wind means.
Turning the electricity off
in one mighty blow, so that when you wake
all the clocks are wrong
and the copper-tube wind chimes
where once I heard a secret
revealed in their music
are splayed in silence,
a dead language in the snow,
waiting to be rehung in the maple.

WHAT'S POETRY LIKE?

Poets play the winter tarantella
making love in the midnight hours
on a white iron bed like a dog skeleton
distinguishing the essential and unessential
moment, shared between ordinary lunatics
and screaming over a bird in an apple tree
until an elegy must be written
to resuscitate the relation.
Those who look
toward the depleted wildlife of neighborhoods
with tragic relish, to see somehow ourselves
disappearing about ourselves.

Once, in New York City, years ago,
the internet technician finally arrived.
His teenage apprentice stood in my living room
over a Tranströmer book. He said it looked
kind of cool, and he wanted to know
what it was. Poetry, I said.
What's poetry like? he asked. And
the treacherous inadequacy with which one
finds oneself explaining in a few loose
deficient words something with lungs
and no face, the immortal freak
of language you haunt and hunt
which is the original state of language
you're trying to get back to from within—
poetry, whose rare geniuses come
as bittersweet suicidal explosions
on the tongue, randomly felt during

long tedious meals; award-winning and
already forgotten. All the emoting of the
unanalyzable fragments. All the surrender
and detonations of precision
and reckless insight
and reference to hidden wisdom and Coke cans—
conversations across time, and slips
into truth, and obscurity of thought, altogether
blissfully, the form itself at its best strings of dreams
in the waking life,
overlaid like unobserved clothing:
the words that sing
stillness, the silence craved
by perpetual auctioneers—that which is not
the tale of event but itself *an* event—

You know what? Just take the book, I said finally,
pushing it into his hands—

Thanks! he said, and took it away, grinning a little.

But later, with snow in my head and a thunder
in my right eyelid, I was worried, as I was
so dangerously then, about dark, yet-unspoken things
—it frightened me: that shiny black-and-white book
wafting around New York City in the back
of a Time Warner Cable van, waiting to be opened,
waiting to torment him, thinking of it changing his life.

MEMORY PALACE

Every memory palace should have a damp basement
with frozen pipes and mouse bones,
shreds of pink insulation, you dare not enter.
Every memory palace should have
my childhood basement, at the dead end of Elm St.,
with its soft beams and dirt floor
where we stored a mannequin named Greta
who scared us to death every time we went to reset the hot-water tank.
Greta, purchased from Lazarus department store's
closing sale, 1996. The same store where my feet
were measured by those amazing people
who used to kneel in front of you
to press a big toe through the leather and tell you to
walk around a little, see how it feels.
Everything khaki and ketchup red; frosted glass, pastel floral.
Santa Claus lived there, at the top of the staircase,
and I sat on him, suddenly aware of how grubby
my winter coat was, and my fingernails; how crooked
my gaze. Greta watched—flawless, in her prime
in the newest sweater and pantyhose and pencil skirt,
not knowing she would be purchased by *us*
for $40. Not knowing she would end up
on the muddy basement of a farmhouse,
naked, dismembered, her breasts bared for no one
but the spiders, the red efts, the plumbers,
her arm lying beside her, her hand
with three missing fingers that were
kicking around somewhere upstairs—

I have no memory palace.
I have tomato paste cans bloated
on a sagging plywood shelf.
Memory: the botulism exhibit. Lockjaw.
A declawed cat. Come, and you'll trip over a cement statue
of a cement bag that got wet before it was even opened,
all its creases preserved perfectly—

when I look back
there's an axe in my head, and tarp draped over it.
There's a white mask hanging on the wall
and no eyes, just holes with more wall looking out,
so angry it's frozen in a red smile, guarding
what can neither see nor hear.

CIVILIZATION AND ITS DISCONTENTS

There are two apple trees in my yard
and I am thinking of what it means
to be alive in this world,
the pleasures of secrecy
living among the florae
I bow low from a professional training
and citizenry of loneliness
to the dark red apples, the wasps
on the ground.
I remember one of my friends
who said he went to the Humane Society
and told them I'll take the dog
no one else wants. A beautiful red hound
could be found leaping around
in his truck cab, barking at everything.
One day that friend left class
and never came back—angry
at something someone said I think
or maybe just tired, as I so often am,
of the whole effort of scrutinizing the dream.

But I like the look of the rawhide antennae,
the tilted femurs,
the dangling empty cocoon husks
and warty lichen specimen
that cover the apple trees.
Last year, only three apples
were born between them
and they grew high up where
no one could reach. Not one blossom

did I see. Only ticks that leapt
onto the thick summer grass
and on our necks.

The quiet of trees is like the quietest girl in gym class
standing against the retracted bleachers,
a moldy copy of Freud's
Civilization and Its Discontents in her hands,
in which a hand-written receipt to her dead father
is tucked into section two as a bookmark.

When the wind blows I stand very still
and hold up a tiny plastic wand.
Bubbles scatter across the yard for my daughter to chase—
she herself said she was a dog
that kept escaping my leash,
returning and growling, getting just close enough
for me to almost catch
so she could escape again.

I wanted to play but I was troubled
by a line I'd written almost ten years ago
and had published—it's too late
to change it now. When you write
you try to make sure it's ready
before you serve it
that at its center it isn't raw
with a bloody spot at the tip
of a pale artery, slopping into prose
whose very nature can be
to think it can clarify
the insoluble fragment—
it's so tempting,

when considering the suffering,
to go prose. To speak of it like that.
I want to defend against the old habit.
I want to get it not *right*, but near.
Speaking a little freely about nothing
or the way roots go down
as our beliefs do among a secret,
while above we make a strange theory
we cannot get right. But
give me a poem, I ask my daughter.
Her pause like a river: wide, fresh and coppery off the mountain.
the trees are flying to the poetry!, she says at last,
and rushes on.

O OF THE FLESH

I dreamed there was
a restaurant
called *O of The Flesh*
we're all meeting up there later
go online and order
what you want
in advance
the password to do so is
fastoftheinnocents
all lowercase
when you write it
implied will be
the actual password
hidden
within that word
all I know is that
it contains two *d*'s
I do not think
it will work
if we know

WRITING CONFERENCE

It was too dark to see the lake.
Write twenty sentences about the lake.

I fell asleep dreaming of the flood again.
Waking to a little broom
sweeping tears over my face.
I was being led to the podium to give a speech.
I was being given a final meal.

I was eating my croissant at a discreet window
and I felt, for the first time,
blameless for being born and contemplating suicide
by black sunflower, red bathrobe belt, the sky—

But it is necessary to die
each day, each moment.
Prepare, that's my advice.

I ask you now, audience of one
billion bored conference members,
why does the most prosaic statement come to us
when we are at the most interesting part
of the execution?

When I say the word *forgiveness* whom do you think of?
The federal loan department
or the insomniac patient
consumed by the grisly possibility of success?

Now write twenty more lines
about the beauty of this world.

THE STUDENTS SINGING BEFORE A FLOOD

I can hear them downstairs
where I left them after breakfast
in the discourse, in the work.

The poem will come
          when one part of you fades and another clarifies.

It will come for the universal
and forgotten conversation, barely legible

          and famous with implicit sound.

I can hear them go on, deconstructing
the autobiographical persona
          from its routine in the room
from its terrible idea of itself.

But then quiet—so long it seems, an outline
          of a pause is almost solid, almost I go to them—
then a guitar begins.

The students from far away, now together,
are singing Fleetwood Mac's "Dreams," quietly, then louder,
they are harmonizing
          while the sky outside unfolds in yeasty clouds
that obscure and uncover the light

and soon it will rain away the roads
exposing steep precipices, the disquieted
underground, the ragged roots

and sheep will have to be
        hoisted into canoes tied to Stop signs

and all the books will swell and warp
and have to be thrown out

and the long milky summer rain
        will keep on falling and falling
like madness

like the white eyelashes of a Clydesdale horse
it will drown the eyes,

a wall of stones
smashing downstream
        will pull the wild grapes out
along the riverbanks—

There was something I wanted.

I was thirsty. I saw the woods.
I saw one velvety slug with its narrowing head
        lying in a clutch of tiny dark green mushrooms
so utterly paused
        and alive I grew
supple and humble to see.

        All that time love was growing dark
in my mouth
and in the body of a song.
        I'm already gone, I thought.

And singing salutes nothing with itself.

Singing comes up through the floorboards
and builds
and overflows at my feet
with its flotsam: car tires and plastic jugs,
smooth limbs of trees, pale and skinned of all bark.

Ever since I was young
a certain sound crept toward me.
Seeped like a gas, a heat's mirage. I gathered it to me and inhaled;
I embalmed myself with it.

Nothing moves but that song they sing.

A mind who has lost its body
must be all sound, mustn't it?

Rushing over its own bones in a frenzied search—
a mind that wanted what it couldn't have.

I think whatever god placed matter here
and cored us
for its liquor to run through

must sit everywhere watching
to see what happens—must look upon us
to see itself
not know itself.

THEODICY

Rut marks
where something was parked,
the grass pale, a rectangle
not seen
in nature.

Where is your RV?
Where pipes
the blackwater?

Where now
your powerful engine
that moves all?

Now we are run through
by feeling
as by a bayonet—

where is the dog
barking
in the distance?

Where the object is
everywhere
you are not,

O impossible otherness
of which we are made.

•

O World, our realm of the tiny relief.

THE TRANSLATION ELEGIES

> Who shows a child as he really is? Who sets him
> in his constellation and puts the measuring-rod
> of distance in his hand? Who makes his death
> out of gray bread . . . ?
>
> RAINER MARIA RILKE, "THE FOURTH ELEGY,"
> TRANSLATION BY STEPHEN MITCHELL

In the gray November birthday light
    of Rutland, Vermont, followed by a newspaper
headline of a child, heard by neighbors
    screaming in an abandoned building all night, far off;
dead in the hospital. The gleeful tabloid keeps you
rubbing the old war wound. You're

shuffling into the familiar perfume of McDonald's
    to get a little sack of fries, black coffee,
like those before you, to sit by the window

    reading the lewd graffitied bathroom stall of your psyche
in November gray angel food cake lit sprawl-light

while your own child climbs into a bright blue tube
        in the play area and disappears
in her halo of static-electric hair.

You are considering again
    something terminal in your personality.
That which cannot be uttered
    or changed. But you're comforted

in that they say every generation
has its own translation of Rilke's elegies,
        belched up upon the shores of Nineveh
out of the mouth of the whale

        to preach to the fallen, the lost—

Rilke, returning, a little changed each time, to us,
if only to attempt to articulate the question
        of why the innocent suffer, why
we cannot gain our innocence back.

        If only to speak into the harrowing space left by a child,
speak with the sour cry of the violin
        whose music loosens and drifts out a window

to slip into the inhaling body below—

we need relief from the constant ricochets of the past!

The unspeakable humiliation of every relationship.
I mean,
        this is all of humanity we're talking about.

Not the chosen affected few, the precious piglets
        trotting behind the cannibalistic sow of sorrow—

all people, slinking to the
        catastrophically informative
mirror. Waiting for a Mephistopheles
        to take on more clients; preparing to go
way, way, way down,
into hell, clutching a little gold key,
                hoping to be one of the ones

who come back up: the returned.

        Staring hauntedly at the exit.
But face flooded with light   and knowing, and gold bees,
warbling around the skull like the treble notes

of a child's screams—
        screams coming from far away—   screams

that are always relative
        to our ability to hear them,
                even if they're "right under our noses,"

even if they're "coming from inside the house—"

It's all Relative, see? like a pill is relative

        to the cosmic nerve.
The intensive short-term psychodynamic epic
is relative to an eternity

of living one way, in your head, and forgotten.

A whole collective consciousness stretching back
to the first suicidal worm, moving happily
        on its circuitous path in the dirt.
And all the while
        God blowing his squealing recorder of silence

in between each word;
he's waving cheerily

through every pore

of those monstrous noses we were under—

you consider that you should throw yourself down
at the bunioned feet of anyone
who comes your way.
Or at least the child—bright, open,
the one waiting loyally for you to
"work it out" so she can get loved already,

should you return in time
from the long and benumbed spectacle
of historic grief.

THOUGHTS AT THE GRAVE

I am considering a stone.
Even alone I feel I am in another performance.
Even the near world is distant.

Certain graves have no headstone, no name,
no dates, no epitaph. Only a good boulder
hauled over with a backhoe
and marked with a twisted wind chime.

Who is it down there?
In the softening box, your discarded limbs,
the unstrung toy with ruthless hair
morphing to wild blue phlox scattered above you.
But for some artfully yellowed dentures

fallen back into the gritty skull
the color is gone as any Grecian statue's now—
as a seashell far from the sea;

I think a ghost follows me—it's not you. It's Nothing.
No-body. I coax her now, here,
where end-of-summer light sleeps
dappled on cots of ground ivy leaves
and ferns sleep awake the border at a
laid-down life—

Some stones are better uncarved, I think.
Uneaten by tool. Even Rodin must have sensed it.
How when a face emerged out of nothing
in his obsessive *work*, that what was hidden
in the stone was lost, once it was carved into something.

How, when a face looks out,
staring from a pedestal, it's stuck seeing.

Rodin, one of his last sculptures was a half-finished bust
of an impatient pope. He threw his apron down in a rage
at the suggestion of using photographs

and limped down the pontifical steps
with tears in his eyes
and died soon after—all that intense *staring* he did

at spiral snail shells,
at the Gothic cathedrals in France,
bombed to rubble, back to the mute stone—

all the observing, which worked its way
into what seemed so like a woman's thigh,
or the vein in a furrowed brow—

but even wind and water
carve stone with their howling gaze.

I see them at the brook, across the yard from here,
where I walk from the grave—I see them
working, working the stone,
pouring into a concaved nothing—

and everyone knows even a slow drop of water
will eventually
create madness, and change,

on a surface—consciousness
that cuts as it goes
paths of solitude into new rooms

and wakes us up, and finds a mirror
and thinks: This is my face.
And it once looked upon yours.

MOTHER'S DAY

There is no succor here. Plus, we have unfortunately denied your application. Though there were many strong moments—one line was quite wry and vulnerable, and in general we liked the nature imagery. (We'll paste in some examples of what was working well.) We wish we could give you money so you might find a quiet gazebo to write more of the same ambiguous and tormented poetry about the same vague abuses no one will give you a medal for since eventually *you liked it,* to be locked in a box the size of an earth, a billion children vying for one cold leftover breast, turning in a soundless dark—

Oh it's hard to console you when you are like this! Out there in wherever you are, drinking from a jar and eating your nightmarish chocolate flower—when you reapply (which I know you *will*) tell them I sent you. Tell them I agreed with you on that one line that said God hides in the transference and no one asks to be born.

ANALYSAND

The fantasies are tangled up
in the old objective suffering.
I'm tired. Just let me sleep.

The anger wears you
until you're blown away
by the slightest breeze—

I've worked so hard, Self.
Now let me sleep.

The archetypal defenses with the hidden feeling—
my body is leathered with them.

I've been rooting around like a truffle pig in the black soil
and the scent on the wind is delicious and rare.
Now let me go, Rapunzel!
You who barely lift your twenty-foot braids!

But there she goes again
letting down her hair for the witch to crawl back up,
to kiss the girl on the lips, to make dark red marks
across her sealed mouth—

When will it end?
Well. There's not much to be done
in terms of thinking it through
it'll start thinking *you*.
Memory is tricky. An issue of the translator.

Memory, rolled in desire like raw meat
in breadcrumbs and yolk, sizzled for ages—
it usually gets worse. Much worse.
Burned beyond recognition in front of everyone.

You must spend as long as it takes
to bear a single word beside another word.

You must find some current event in your gaze.
You must look up
at the eternal stranger
there, in an intimacy
you'll never see the top or the bottom of
just the navel
of the dream—

and he'll approach and stand
at a distance
that profits not
but for the work
and you must love

and make him cry
at least once, your little drama
flayed on the cross in front of him,

you must play it out
and then spend hours alone in its aftermath
looking out the window,
watching the sky change in one day,

watching hawks circling in it—so high they're like
barrettes, matter, caught
in the blowing gray hair
of a great and bodiless mind.

THE TEMPTATION OF SAINT ANTHONY

In the paintings his face is often averted, turned upward
toward the always unclear God
or staring at the creature composed
of animal and human parts

or else he is staring straight ahead, as if at us,
the supposed viewer and
he appears to be drowning
surrounded by a gleeful orgy,
a corpse with spindly legs and nubbed feet
rearing over him—they *perform* for him.
The Queen of Sheba, with her coterie
she comes holding an enormous, illumined manuscript,
opened for him
reflecting light from an unknown source,
no doubt filled with esoteric knowledge—
and still he resists.

But what he sees not, we see.
The elephant with a woman hanging off its trunk, men in striking profile,
slobbering mouths, everything pleading for dick,
for the dick of the eye for Christ's sake!
They want in. And we're in.
The translucent shawl over the naked body
gathered in skilled drapery
like butter raked over with a fork—

Pity no rage at the light.
Pity no whore at your feet, who is you!
Pity no monkey holding a plum to the mouth
of a stripped-down world—you stripped the world

when they stripped you into it
and you knew you would go out and strip them for it,

your need enchained to a legendary need
and you went stripping the eyes
off the heads of your dolls
went tearing your eyes out of the I's,
your joy, that which is graver than,
and lonelier than,
anything else—
you locked into a stare, and went tearing the iris—
well, now . . .

What he sees not, we see.
What he sees, we see not.

And we're watched by a pig
with a little bell around its neck.
And ever the man at the center is there—

He is no Narcissus who will not be touched.

He might look up and say,
It's not really about me, is it?
And you might admit, No. It's not really about him.

It's about painting and change and stillness.

The transference of light, making
the moon seem halved, and your tortured nothing, your invisible
charge you stand before,

        the event of it all, curative and more violent
than the narrative of your life will ever be.

The contextual, with its symbolic marginalia,
drifts around your skull.

You keep waking up with a moth eating a green sun,
you keep waking up trapped,
the aporia, without the metaphor—but looking at the paintings

until you notice in one
a stag, standing and staring from the distance
of the so-called background.

Backgrounds *see* the fore and seem to know
something else.

And beyond that, another background . . .

Surely some art historian could explain this!
The way the unseen gets in
and stares back at you.

Like you can reach a status of zero.
There, but only implied.

See how he sits beside a vanitas skull, and his book,
    for in his restraint
he has grasped another world.

THE MASK

The mask won't laugh,
no matter how well you deliver the lines.
At this point (you must admit)
it might not ever open its lips.
Yet it lives this whole life in your head . . .
You could both be understudy. Unclear
who stars. Cue the door being shut.
The pillow put over your face.
Hog-tied and brushed bald
into a lifelong blackout in every scene—

Oh, can't sleep either?
Here, take these two little white pills.
One's the moon, the other
the reflection of the moon
on the cold water of a November lake.
One will make you howl,
the other remain silent—
same moon, see?

The knocking, the knocking . . .

Why don't you tell me a joke.
Tell me that one about John
fighting his way to the
muttering Jesus on the cross,
who is calling for him to come—
I'm coming! John says, but with each attempt,
a limb is chopped off by the Romans
until finally the rolling limbless body

arrives below the blessèd feet
of the Son, who looks down, croaking
John! Oh John—look, look!
I can see your house from here . . .

II

If we arrive at the house, we arrive knowing we've been here before. Memory's imagination dreams what is. In the first seeds of what would become his film *Mirror*, Tarkovsky kept dreaming the same dream of his childhood home, as if he were walking into it but not into it, around it all the time. He believed the dream carried some fact, some sense, something very important, for why should a dream pursue a man so?

The film opens with a stuttering boy. His face tics; a tic on the eyelid; the knock, the knockings—he is trying hypnosis. A woman in Russian says: look at your hands, Yuri. Concentrate! On the count of three they will become immobile, Yuri—*look at me!* I am going to lift this *transfixion*, and you will be able to speak clearly, freely, easily, and articulately. You will be able to use your hands and your voice, loud and free! she says.

Black and white, the world seems at once. The work of a turned-away God in the overgrown field before the woods, and the house, where a mother smokes. She runs toward a letterpress machine to see if a terrible, unknown word has been mistakenly published. She laughs with anguished relief to see it is still hidden. We spring in and out of color, and the mother spills her purse upon the floor. My own mother is a silence so profound I forget the hair-raising scream it punctuated. Like living in a constant state of being woken by something, but not knowing by what: frozen and listening, hearing only your own battering heart. The mother is closely watched, like fire: the first mirror, the first object, the first house, burning.

Does it make sense to prove something? Let's see . . . you have a photograph here. Known images. The historical someone. She's seven years old, standing in the snow after dark in her best dress, betraying a grubby white tennis shoe, staring into the camera. The communal, unsmiling, and desperately loved child, stepping out of the immortal Thanksgiving dinner and into the mortal Thankstaking fast. The distant sounds of laughter in the house. The cold, making her clutch her shoulders, arms across her chest like the dead's, laid out at the end—but alive, clung to, here, in the photograph, in a hand, at a beginning.

In the beginning was a word.
You suspect the word was *No* . . .
"The loveliest word in the dictionary," Dickinson had said.

In the beginning was a word.
Then it needed two people to think about it.

Who could cut a word open?
The wind chimes said their secret
was that they held a secret; the wind blew through them and they touched indifferently.

•

How can we grasp the ungraspable? is always the question. How can we inscribe experience that never knows the whole? I know love wanted to go through me, but there was a wall covered in misspelled swear words, reddening of ivy, a lead flap with no knob to open it.

In the mirror I looked at someone else. When I touched myself, I met only rain. Forgive me, I'm not even here. Gone as the worm; gone as the body of Echo, as the body of Narcissus—only the res-erection of a yellow, narcotic old-world lily, Wordsworth's inward eye, the daffodil in my skull, the cock rubbed upright by the sun.

•

What is sound in the dream? An idea? What is the dream with a dreamer there? What is the dream that cannot dream, or think, but itself? An utter ceaselessness, a rich nothing. A chowder of white on white— I want to look upon the face of someone who sees suffering and stands it, utterly still, patient and hidden.

This field of the human soul! The one with God's hoofprint in it, the one he galloped through! The one evident place, a libidinous field, around a black house.

LINE RECEIVED FROM AN INTIMATELY UNKNOWN SOURCE

It's never meant to be literal
and each piece is meant to be shared.

IN SHADOW, WHO MADE THESE WORDS

"All poets are liars," my play begins.
Plato was probably right. With this enfeebled mind
my only recourse is poetry.

Behind my head, heads begin to nod.
They doze in the surgical amphitheater behind my eyes.

I do not know what I hold more clearly in my mind:
the pain of what I had
or the pleasure in what I don't.

In the afterlyric of childhood
you can barely stand to look back
without laughing

at how calmly desire and memory
see fit to destroy everything.

And thank God!
Let me be run through
with the wooden javelin of truth.

Let them remove my breastplate and grille
and wipe the mud from my brow.

Let them place a rose in my hand
and mutter that old prayer
and wave two fingers over me.

Let my only work be this,
to stare back
into the blue iris of the sky.

I'll continue to do my best. Nevertheless, I hear you can drown in two inches of water. Will anyone notice if I drown in my espresso? Looking down I see the reflection of an eye staring back up at me, wavering in the tiny white cup, like a black sunflower. What if you looked upon the world and the world looked back? Frightening. I'm weary of being in charge of own misery. I give some of it to you to decipher. I'm here rereading the same one page from Goethe's *Faust* until it reads me.

•

Do you only want to hear what you've heard before? No. Whatever comes; whatever comes, I find my gold key.

UNSENT LETTER

I love this view of the trees along the cliff out my window. (I'm having some alone time.) The leaves have fallen, so you might see high school students running the winding trails in the woods during gym, a thrashing ponytail on a svelte quarterback, he's leading the track-and-field girls to Deadman's Corner. Do you recall 2016, November, Chappaqua wilderness, walking slowly in a long, embroidered coat? Sometimes one fantasizes about a sturdy stick, finding some semblance of peace, giving up the game, living quietly. And I should follow suit. As always, I'm considering suicide.

I'm here every Monday, folks!

I crush it. I leave to thunderous applause, weeping audience members, mobbed book table, back door exit, $100 honorarium. I amble out to the parking lot and weave home. I wander the highway with the dog, as if from a horror film: dazed, tender to the touch, shimmering cheeks. Come back to us! my husband says. He holds my shoulders, shakes me a little, like something sedimented, a snow globe with a woman walking in a white blizzard to a tiny black house at its center.

DYAD

I resent not being able to quit without serious, generational, catastrophic backlash. So. I come to you live, via satellite, from the black house, with an old sentence stitched back together on my wrist, barely audible; I come as killer of gray, the wielder of black & white, to split down the middle, swing wildly at the hoarfrost light—I do as my ancestors did: idealize and devalue the average beloved. I abandon you; I betray your body. I come to you as someone bitten during a yellow moon, marred forever by the adored wolf—but when I say to the analyst: I don't know what I'm doing! and he says, *Bullshit*—we watch the soul leap up and through; guilty, and powerful with such a glue, it vibrates the gorge of minds, and, for a moment, welds the unlike two.

THE TOPOGRAPHY OF THE UNSEEN

To be suicidal is understandable considering the circumstances.
The whole rasping tumultuous human history
punctuated with beauty and burdock.
We must distill it to a syrup in the sugarhouse.
See the resident Übermensch unpinning tears from little spikes in the brain
and leading them on gold chains to the eyelid.

I heard from the black sunflower you can drown in two inches of water.
What if you cried a two-inch ocean and threw yourself in?
I often think that. Water is always held, bordered, contained.

It can wait, or be let go of, under the condition of
the uttered word—the body's departure
or its immanence of return.

KNOW THY OTHER

The analyst is an imposing metaphor of the exterior. He is the ultimate eroticism: all looking with no touching. Yet, given time to be oneself, untouched, one suddenly touches the self. What Narcissus could not achieve, his hand disturbing only water, wanting to penetrate what is nowhere.

•

I do not know what I hold more clearly in my mind:
the pain of what I can never have,
or the pain of knowing
I have its equivalence, which is a shocking
contrast, a kind of magnificent reality.

What do you do with what you have?
Some ancient blackout that's still covering everything
like an immaterial theater troupe's curtain—

I am speaking of course
of love.

AN HOUR

What can you really do in it?
Condense the metaphor further?
Glimpse God beyond the atom?
It isn't a question.
It's an official statement.
So shifts the blurry tattoo.

That teardrop didn't seem to be going anywhere quickly.
A key clutched in your hand,
coat still on, ready to run out the door,
start the car and peel off down Route 7
toward the marble quarry.

But the falling failing temporal
dish of it keeps arriving;
time keeps arriving,
time keeps serving itself,
steaming on a huge platter.

Every second is a death: irretrievable,
gone, made past.

Every second a death one second
and a resurrection the next.

And between each, the split second, and so on and so on,
infinite in its never-wholeness—

The other body behind his body
was whispering
something obscene.

Now that I have you:
whom do you see when you look at my face?

What did she do over her long, stunned vacation? Reality, then reality. It came to her, as the fierce trumpet of September's blue sky comes, above an overripe-bluets fall. She told it—like a confession not her own. Her brother had helped her kill a man, she said. And they cut up the body, and they buried its parts all over the small town. "Right under everyone's noses" by the hardware store, and in the bakery's flower beds, under the grade school lawn. There was an unspoken agreement to never speak of it; only for her alone to recall, years later, in horror—her alone to realize surely some body parts would be found, eventually, by someone. And with this thought came an equally horrible realization that some parts would never, ever be recovered, no matter how hard anyone looked, and this included the head.

There was a pause. The allotted oceanic minutes and the waves were nearing their end. Soon, it would be time for the next person. Or how long it had been? Her mouth was dry; she felt exhausted. The audience, she realized, looking up, seemed happy. Its one, attentive face. Confessions of reality's reveries breed silence. She looked out the window at a dead tree by the road. A snag she thought it called: leafless and dried out, smoothed white like driftwood from the wind. It was twisted into uncanny points, and four vultures, huge and motionless, perched there. One was shifting and opening its wings so that wind could cool in between the glossy, dark brown feathers. Then unmoving, with its wings spread wide, it loomed, like night in the sun; it glared down on the Dollar General.

Fall staggered on, beautiful and stung from battle. I strode with it, among the dried lace sleeves on the withered arms of goldenrod, the wrecked husks of milkweed pods, their purses pulled inside out, their gossamer silk tassels with flat brown seeds on the end snagged on the velvety green barbs of the pod's lip—and I studied it all, the color of what fades, the used-up lust. I looked into empty birds' nests with their gray dappled guano below, the rotted tomatoes red, and yellow, like flaccid breasts in the unweeded garden beds—and I'll admit I looked with longing for the hushed, the passed on, the dead.

And what makes a man talk to someone as if their little life mattered at all? I asked myself, as I raked the yard around my house with a bloodshot eye—what makes one person care about another's life? This one life, this one life . . . I'd ask out loud, running a troubled finger along my jaw, unable to leave, too restless to sit in front of the TV—and I'll admit I considered my own autumnal end more seriously than before. I'll admit having arrived at something, I wanted nothing. I'll admit it was different, the way my whole body felt stunned back to a terrible burn. The way a bright red door took me like Jove. To think of being changed to something else! To be a white ox, the cat, a lilac bush, to be changed to a seagull, ignored, or thrown fries outside McDonald's, to be set as a mute perennial. Or to be a revelation of Tiresias, come to its end—to be Pentheus's blood, staining the woods, staining his mother, and his aunts who, in a ritual frenzy, tore his cloaked body apart, spiked his masked face on a stick, and danced it in the dark back to the city, to his father's feet—oh to be a forecast, cast and done.

YOU DON'T KNOW HOW LIPS BURN

To be, all day, haunted by the porn star with the scars on her thigh, disturbed on a couch, upside down; so seems the world—

I don't have time for this!
I have work to do.
A family to feed. Life calls to me.

Life sounds like a vacuum
pulled back and forth
in the next hotel room.

I don't have time for the archaic hatred
stirred awake by love.

We need a new national holiday.
One where we can sit all day at the kitchen table,
eat Depression cake
and struggle with the problems of art.
How it seizes on whatever occasions life offers
and enhances the constructed object.
How it works for something else.
How it cannot be stopped.

The people want a day set aside for deep-dive criticism to be dived.
They want to read Paul de Man, to read out loud the line:

> The alternating feeling of attraction and repulsion
> that the romantic poet experiences toward nature becomes
> in Mallarmé the conscious dialectic of a reflective poetic consciousness—

and then burp loudly.
They want to say the word *fungible,* slow and sexy,
to the golden retriever on the couch. They want a morning
spent masturbating at the window to the bird feeder,
listening to Miles Davis's "You Don't Know What Love Is,"
a few bittersweet tears falling, chocolate and olive oil
on their breath—coming with the redtail hawk's cry.

SPRUNG FROM NOTHING

Last night I saw suddenly the emptiness of shadow, both its void and negation—and simultaneously how full it was: of bones and nests, of fertilizer and blood and substance broken down, a brew for life, turning into a concave that alternated as a protruding point, a nipple, the one that inspired the Virgin Mary's unicorn to spring out of nothing, no doubt. A shock of feeling went through me for this contrast. It is the first, the original. We hold the singular shadow in us, the deep m-other, the cosmic, looking at itself—God is in the black house.

PEELE'S *NOPE*

for Ian

What can a frame hold but the galloping, the galloping, haunted spectacle; a record in a certain way. To capture the entertainment of entertainment of pain. The proof, the witnesses, the history and erasure and repetition, and the dead's deadly pocket change in the rain. There is a hidden room behind his room, made to hold the secret room, of trauma displayed behind glass, behind a door, the preserved fragments. How long will you keep it there? Frozen on its pedestals. The drop of blood on a sneaker; the animal forced into clothes—the laugh track, the libidinous steed. There was a meager veil over the scarred and eaten face.

The consequence of voyeurism is that the object might take revenge. The stalking vacuum comes to suck it all into the torture womb. To belch it back up onto the childhood house, paint it over in blood. Until the prey stalks from room to room, methodically, with the machete, musical, raging past horror. And the siblings want proof. Of something unseen they've seen, in a blue desert sky, with its stemless flower and appetite. How do we move on from the appetite of others is the question. If I cry out, who will come but the monstrous angel in its camouflage of mirrors? And what is it to have proof of that which haunts us? I think I am done with proof. Done with my Oprah shot. The grief is the proof.

I return from the film. I go to my room at the top of my own house—I can see everything except the house itself. The house is the ultimate object. It says you have all the proof you need. It says there is no moving on, there is only a kite, and a letting go. It says you must live with this.

BELIEF

The briar patch where I was born is flowering.
A stone path leads to the brook.
Hummingbirds find the greensward's stargazer lilies,
their sepals open like the intimate eye of new belief.

Yes. I would.
If I died today.
I would repeat this life.

LIRIOPE'S POEM

Can you see how hard Self works to undo what
has been done? My son, Narcissus, was beautiful from the seed
forced into me by the river.
He, too, was in a doomed autonomy.
Boggy field of happiness—forgive me. I was dreaming
of the flood again—

Tiiiime to wake down! Someone sang,
moving in the room,
flinging open the blinds—holding coffee,
Tiresias, again
with his backward news.
It makes me scared, but it's okay, he says,
unfolding his new words with care:

It's never meant to be literal
and each piece is meant to be shared.

If ye enter here, ye may never leave. And if ye leave, ye must leave through a red door into the chilly grass. The driveway is long and no one walks to the mailbox anymore: they creep, they forget, they dance a little to shake off thought. And if anything is worth writing down it is written between comparisons—let it live there in the liminal wasteland, remembering how eventually Virgil had to go, and Dante had to go on.

What is suffering toward something? Condemned to Hell with its willows, where the suicides wait for a cut to be made in the bark; a mouth to call out from, to let loose a shriek—eternal punishment is withheld grief.

•

There is a beauty in the measuring of time. I'm in the musk rose garden, touched by all that love and crime. Full of seemingly limitless *tears*—an "ocean of tears," the analyst said, when they arrived Hegelian over their threshold of snow to flood. Can anyone *describe* the past without similes of depth? Bachelard wondered. Even the soul in its old life was deep-sea.

Eventually nothing is weeping anymore—not the sky with its ladle of darkness; not the analyst with his museum keys, sleeping in his city, in his hidden totality. Only here, in the intactness of a fragment.

•

I saw a wide, cavernous lake in the night. I saw the wise, ruined child with the dark hair. Now beside her appeared an old, male loon, bird whose red eye looked out from his velvety black-and-white-feathered head. The two stood a moment in silence, a weird couple—those who never spoke, but occupied everything. There was a hut nearby, a light burning, a plain wooden cot, and not a single book anywhere. I went in and I slept in that austere room. One life, this one life—it is all so near. I abandoned. I held. I returned. I heard the waves. And hearing the waves, I dreamed back the world.

III

How can a distance be so unendingly near
yet not come any nearer—not all the way?

RILKE, "FROM TIME TO TIME . . .",
TRANSLATION BY FRANZ WRIGHT

THE AFFLUENCE OF BEING

A gold wreath spins at the core.
Glass-beaded, the soul swings from the nose.
Fine-tooled leather flies apart and together when walking.
Minute loops of brass, chain mail gowns,
draped on, hide nothing.
Yellowing ivory piano key teeth
around a wet, velvet tongue. Fire-drop breasts.
Lapis lazuli sentience. Pigment at the fingertips.
Glass fountain frontal lobe, installation of skin.
Lavish brooch on purple mink genitals.
Sand at the corners, full-length cheering mirror,
parody of time, sharp cold inhale
on a Christmas-morning dawn. The patina,
the verdigris, the grassy pits, tarnished smile and the yawn.
The mortal bone-china clavicle kissed.
Pilled silk eye bone. The hallowed hand-hewn beam
of the cock. The thistledown, milk and lilac, cherry
or amethyst, veins of coal, book of the vagina,
perfectly tuned strings of weeping, and soul's cello
moan, in the handset type of time—
O matter of the world!—water and butter and wine!

TRYING TO MAKE SENSE IS THE WORSE MADNESS

This is your final song, Gleeman.
Go on and quit this. Time for a bow,
out the room, bottom first, head last;
out the swinging curtains, stumbling backward
and wondering forever: are they still there?
Waiting for encore? Or am I
quite alone . . . hidden-hidden
masked, in the dark,
and no one is coming.
Surely the flowers are coming,
hitting the heavy draperies,
falling with a whisper to the floor
like a bra, a dog settling. But
little fists flailing too,
thump wildly in the enormous
sweaty chest of Who Is Speaking,
dancing out there around the obvious,
you there, in your dog-hair-covered black overcoat,
the stare near-far-unsighted,
didn't Mother say after begging you
to sing that new ballad, Speak *clearly*.
Why don't you speak clearly the words
you're saying? But then there you are
mumbling still, tongue lopped off
by her rotary cutter and sewn
into the family crazy-quilt—no wonder
the crowd got up
awkwardly and shuffled out
sideways down each isle
while you stood backstage

in a frozen pose—exactly like the man
on the open-door psych ward
who, when asked why he stood contorted
and upright in the middle of his room
for hours, said he was trying to
work backward through a thought—
his days searching the city dump
for a scrap of his baby blanket,
driven there every morning
by a guilty nurse,
and picked up at dusk.

Where are my manure-matured white lilies now?
O heart! O heart!
You pound and pound!
The risk was huge, my heart!
And I am pulling you out of a plastic bag
again, I am hurtling you
through the dark;
soon you will land
triumphantly at their feet
with a splat.

RUPTURE

I'd thought
since everything ends in fire
as surely as it began
and space is cold
dark and light
at the same time
so silent
and unforgiving
I'd thought I'd make a big show
of leaving
to hell with it
God can warm his ass
on Armageddon
I'm done
all that screaming
crying, that hysterical laughter
those nightingales on the screen
the humiliation of the human world
will keep going and going in space
with no object to absorb it
within me, within me
I know Armageddon
is there
as is the olive grove
with its bitter black fruit
and the door with its
yin-yang doorknob

and I return to you now
in ragged bandages

I come back
an antichrist in July
standing in the yard
with my haunted Weedwacker
its five ground-nesting sparrow chicks
circling, translucent
fledging finally
in death

WHAT IS THE BIOLOGICAL FUNCTION OF WORDS?

Why are they a river with no beginning or end
or mother—who turns out to be
just another human, another condemned passenger
at the water's edge and her soft brown antlers
the shadow of a thought.

What are words to dancing? Which is said to be
indicative of feeling happy, playful, and free.
I can't really argue with that, except
I recall Betty Boop had to dance
when they shot bullets at her feet. But

not being able to tolerate what you know
you must be willfully ignorant
and your ignorance polished
to a shimmering tumor, pressed against memory,
a labium of sorrow, sorrow's legend,
while a little frog dances
the Charleston, only when no one is watching.

Now go ahead. Come and tell me
I made everything up. Well, maybe I have.
But even that means something.

I always want to say profound things to you.
A dirty thought like a cry at dawn.
Deer in the Queen Anne's lace trample the sward
and part the grass, as summer moves on
under a moon whose light is not even her own—
and words, leading up to something incredible,

lonely, and honest, flowing between the embankments
en route to a colossal event—words
fail me. It's normal to hate words. And phrases, like
He lost the battle against depression, and
Let me be perfectly clear—and yet they come,

my god they come to us like sunlight,
reflecting off volcanoes on the moon,
they come to us like rage, and love,
and disencumbered, they avail.

THE CIRCUITOUS PATH TOWARD INERTIA

If you want to know anything
consider the distance between you
and the dying of things.
One might linger
there in an eros of silence.
If you want to know anything
you must drive an indifferent vehicle
with your difference locked inside it
to a reading in Salem, Massachusetts,
for $100 and dinner and a place to stay.

Your daughter makes two bottle caps wander her lap
in the back seat—she names them each—
and you both sing the song you've
played all September, a piano and a woman's dusky voice
in regret and love, she sings, moving you
in a held agreement
that music cannot be possessed
though it takes over the whole body
with a song of self-destruction
which is its own specific pleasure,
eroded déjà vu;
you are moving fast on the road
winding through the mountains of Vermont
in a heavy traffic, to the same goal,
Freud's death instinct—how he said
what we desire most is to return
to the old state of things
the first stony lifeless form we held,
how we live merely
a circuitous path toward inertia

on a road distinctly repeating itself
on all sides, as this one, with the vertical green slopes
of bowed ferns, a green waterfall,
hiding the ground that is thick with sunk fronds
and tiny curled rinds of insects: the layers of what was once
the incessant clinging, and letting go.

You're happy. You're moving with your child
into a room of willing people,
for language drew you out to back roads
through the mountains, heavy with cars;
at the big turn, where the signal drops,
two turkey vultures are crouched in the lane
pulling at the meat of some run down animal
and you remember something about the original angels
having six wings: two to cover their feet,
two for covering their faces,
and two for flight itself,
carrying important messages for a silent God
while their cries of jubilation were terrible
and their strange ways were performances
of paraplegia, blindness, and deference,
since it was known too
they had names
and strode between men
and God
and their wings were riddled with open eyes.

And you remember how little
you carried messages for yourself,
for so long, and lived as ambassador
of others' pleasures, and suffering
until it became your own—but too

you would pretend to know the notes
on the clarinet in school band
hoping to be overlooked by the conductor
and how you'd stay like that,
closing your eyes,
pretending to be swept up in the notes
until you really were—the reed in your mouth
became the same fever as the mouth
as if it had always been there.

The gaze of the vulture is a downward gaze.
It rises like the earth itself, slow and heavy and dark,
the corpse assimilating within it,
its back to you—you think if you'd seen its face
you would have seen fire there,
and you would have had to stand it,
the wing bones hunched like someone trenchcoated
upon whom a heavy rain is falling.
The deep brown of its feathered form,
now intensified in sluggish urgency, moves
to rise right; while its mate goes left—
it seemed a pregnant woman
getting off the floor after kneeling to pick up a toy,
so slow, its great bulk—the car before you
clips it, and it reels sideways, and falls, trembling.
Undifferentiated, ironic. No shadow but itself.
And you drive on.

THE DECLINE AND FALL OF THE ROMAN EMPIRE

The name of Poet was almost forgotten; that of Orator was usurped by the sophists. A cloud of critics, of compilers, of commentators, darkened the face of learning, and the decline of genius was soon followed by the corruption of taste.

THE HISTORY OF THE DECLINE AND FALL OF THE ROMAN EMPIRE

You must be careful to fall in a certain way.
With the raw embryonic-field-mice thoughts
birthed in the junk drawer and their eyes licked open.
Careful to let loose a scandalous vision
that opens in your head one disfigured wing
and you must attempt to translate
the gray ring, left greasy round the tub of skull
where the ocean was a second before you woke
with its entire word you barely grasped by syllable or sight.

And without pay, too. Amid the throng
whose bite is bored and bottom line and on the hill.
Look not for love from them, but that small return
of distant lyric sent shy and bold across the air
from some reader in their night. Let the few suffice,
if they can return the call.

Alone you hate it all. But write it, write it down!
To up and out; strange thing: a screw in your soul
that goes with nothing, fits nowhere, and yet you build
for years and place it hopefully in each failed book.
And it builds you too—your shabby architecture

going gray and bald, in a shabby chair, your mind
drifting to desire and back, to watching desire
in curiosity; you who make use
of the unthought thought with eaten air
and alone for thee
in doubt and joy and poverty.

UNDERWATER CANDLE

I dreamed the words
underwater candle.

For we are
the golden ass
searching
in the dark
for a rose
to transform
us back
and it takes
time searching
the world
the metaphors
become painful
and we watch them
born in the corpse

Oh cleaners of rot
in that surgical theater
what is the worm to
a golden ass?
Waiting in rigid
torment of the heart
under anesthetic
a gentle silver-winged message
without anything in it—

the message the angels carried
was only

more silence
the blank page

It took all this time
to know that
(*No* that)

to see something move
in the dark
that spread out
behind my eyes

desire and its mascots
the puppets of memory

they appear in different guises
without will
sodomized
as the earth
shamed
the golden ass
braying
under a star
a hole in the ether
a star falling
into the sea
falling and falling
into the beer-dark sea
whistling
burning
burning
even there—
I mean something

surely—
or else not meaning

is so dear to me
like a stuttering child
my underwater candle
inverse universe—
my *No*
my down
my black house
I come knocking
on a fathomless depth
wrapped around
red on the inside of everything
like the inside
of an antique teacup—

Human beings
if we should die
and return
into the ordinary pain
of the autobiographical
would we be okay—would we
exult in joy at knowing
we would do it all exactly the same?
Do I live like that?
As if I would
repeat this life?

ANXIETY OF MEANING

Certain events draw you nearer to meaning.

All poets are liars,
wrecked against meaning, starved
on the beach of meaning—

I want to keep your head in a black bag, I'd said.

Who can distinguish the remembered
from the desired. I know a little
the agony of it. I drew nearer still.

What do I know about getting?
I know my mother turned away.

That I slipped from her body again and again,

tied down in an incubator and punctured
with a lifesaving light.

I know that all that time an ancient poem
was writing itself in the
hallway, where a mask hung on the wall

looking without seeing.

I know I turned away.
Can you feel it?
How the head longs to rid the face
of a certain danceless dance.

That we were
condemned to dualism at birth.
That dualism is dead.
And long live dualism.

That certain events of love
drew us nearer to mean.

That the heart is chilled
by a tormented wave

that thinks it is not the sea.

FRAGMENT

I fear it so, not meaning;
or else

it is so dear to me:
my meaninglessness

I'm so afraid you will take it away,
that which
I long to be rid of—

The implied wish
to stay forever
and leave immediately—

it is a bittersweet sum of reality

ON THE NATURE OF THINGS

Of love I am slowly becoming
more aware. When love manifests from exactly
where it has always been
it fills in my head like a gold crayon.
Lucretius knew love to be suspect.
So the Christians said he was given a potion for it that nearly killed him
and in rare moments of lucidity for his remaining life
he railed against love; always working endlessly
on his stunning, six-volume didactic pagan poem
on Epicurean physics
the nature of existence
and the condition of making the lover
into a godlike power
before he committed suicide.
And for this we consider love's therapy.

Love comes like a wave
but unmoving. It smacks upon the ground
in froths of salt and sand, says *You*
and disappears.

One shivers then.
Love makes you more susceptible to wind.
Of the erotic, forget what you know.
For love leaps along, the unremembered part of the dream.

Love is not memory, it is despite memory.

Who I am? The word *nothing*
always comes to mind.
Dwindling to the great phenomenological drama.

Nothing? I am *nothing*? Say *that* into the mirror
for as many times as it will take
to be onto something.
We go to mirrors to see what nothing manifests as.
Only to find we're still there.
As if cleansed of all misunderstanding of stillness
by its lemon and metal and light
so slow you can barely tell it is happening.

One thinks: I'm ashamed to be alive.
But so what. Even God is a humiliated god!
Dismembered in the moonlight
and pasted back together in the morning
into reason, a word, like he never was.

We cannot even fully recall the *circumstances*
of our own lifetime, and its liars, its lying in the wave,
any more than we can recall who that god of mirrors was,
written to on a wealthy woman's bandages of linen
that no one could fully translate.

Where is the lost thing; where is the note
that divided the beginning—where is the manuscript
Walter Benjamin carried on his person
when he, in despair, killed himself at the border of Portbou,
fleeing Hitler, denied asylum?

The manuscript he'd dragged
through the perilous mountains in a suitcase.
The one his companions called his "burden."
The one he claimed was more important than his life,
and disappeared with his life . . .

In the absences of words consciousness grows wild and green and sentient,
a black sunflower pointed at the sun.
A mind searching for its mind.

Maybe that manuscript is being held somewhere
on a velvet pillow in a glass room
beside a carved jade tongue
and a precious ivory pipe with teeth marks on its tip.
Maybe it's being read by only one man,
over and over again, who weeps every time.
Or, like all matter, it is dissolved,

as all our books one day will be—though
the law of conservation of matter says it's still there!
That something cannot be made into nothing.
And given infinite time it may reconstruct itself,
exactly the way it was, then on and on,
to every known object in existence,
that we're all changing form
and all will return. I can't explain the math.
Staring blankly at ourselves everywhere.
Surrounded by flowering weeds and gray waves,
leaning to drink from a mirror
and unable to look away,
committing suicide by ironic gaze.

What if your suicide poem
was the worst thing you'd ever written?
And of course it is: wrenching and hackneyed and tired.
But nothing really ends.
This thing that flops along the kitchen counter
grabbing at the rinds of sourdough and butter

goes on, ambivalent, tortured with thought,
tongued with the angel's rambling, dissonant chord.

I speak to you now, old lying mind,
in all these short nightmares Valéry called *language*.
I speak to you
who hide, veiled among the image fires
in a body with hair growing gray upon it,

a hand, writing of its hand—I speak from the body,
which hides a child, who is nothing.

THE ANNUNCIATION

for Ben

At the Met I was looking for two
Temptations of Saint Anthony,
but they are stored
in the basement. So I went instead
in search of your favorite motif: the archangel Gabriel
announcing to Mary she would
bear the impossible infant.
I've been trying to describe a sun
for weeks now anyway.
There are so many annunciations
they found *me*, but I searched
for the prized Botticelli.
I finally find it, and it is small
and distinct in its perspective,
the pillars that separate Mary from the angel
present more like a wall
so that each figure seems to be
in their own chamber, a dyad,
on the right and left. She kneels
in her room, while the angel bows in his,
each of their androgenous foreheads are
aligned across the distance
and her bed, which is always there
in the background,
made with tight-fitting linens,
must emphasize
nothing has spent the night
but the light

glittering beams of semen
from outside the room—a consciousness
from beyond them, finding them
in the architecture.

I love to look at what you love to look at.
See how she is alone yet with another?
I long for how she yields,
even in her fear, she yields to it—
distance which
nevertheless
is touch.

OVID

On the sour shores of the black sea
I finished my book.

Unwittingly, this work perceives
how desire changes and suspends things.

I was prefigured by an echo.
That woman quickening in me,
her sound is sound *on* wind
bashing against the grotto wall—

She is not wind. Yet
she raves through ribs and clavicles
the trussed beam of spine she left behind.
She dries the cathedral of my mouth.

It weeps in its way, the wind.
It weeps a flecking spittle
from the black sea,
cold against my cheek.

REALITY 2!

I'm making a documentary called Reality 2!
Everyone we interview
seems to be confined to their body
while Canada geese move
with an image of themselves
moving in their minds above us;
often I point my lens upward
while my subject speaks
mummering of starlings;
I let the wind hit
the microphone
and I keep it so
in Reality 2! I'm interested
in the innate paradoxes
of the human soul.
Joel is making this with me.
We're riffing on his late father's epic poem
of Jason and Medeia, which came to him
in a vivid, continuous dream,
night after night, persisting
until he wrote the whole thing down,
354 pages, opening with Kreon, old and scowling
looking out over the blue-green valley
great dark towers of clouds
piled high with dark ideas
and dancing arrows—
sad and old Kreon, Antigone in the ground,
Oedipus gone and haunting everything—
olives and apples on the wind's breath—
Is it possible to capture this in 60 minutes?

Lighting, the soundtrack, the wardrobe
all coalescing; violinist and trumpeter
at the ready, my old band teacher
his pink face and shock-white hair—
a kind of Kreon himself;
my husband and his annunciation collection
and a close-up of someone
buttering toast with a machete—
a mother smoking;
dirty water floods a toilet bowl,
a woman stands in an overgrown yard
someone eating a chicken carcass with her hands,
and high and deep
the images go
and cruel and pleasurable the cuts
and someone holding on to the silk tassels of a power-source!
We'll fly, God dammit!

The camera pointed at another face,
capable of giving an intense stare
of fierce love
and hatred—

which I was reading about today
sitting in the gazebo
a book in which
the last paragraph
says all one can hope for
finally is
not exactly to be *cured*
but maybe one can be
a little
"sadder and wiser"
at the end . . .

I don't want to be
"sadder and wiser"
at the end.
But I already was.
And one point,
you can't unsee
what you've seen
without being
willfully ignorant.

Anyway, I have my film to finish.
My great experimental documentary
on the innate paradox of the soul.
Being unable to see myself
from within myself
I have to look at you, wherever you are, out there
eating your flowers—
in other words
another person's reality,
to imagine it
and the work that goes into
the velvet baubles
on the buds of a sumac tree
and a white inchworm just born
on my big toe in the grass
and the wind in the hair
of my daughter—
the eyes and fate
of another person—anyone, really—but
one person at a time, really seeing them,
dreaming their reality, *Reality 2!*
Like mine,
but vastly otherwise
and unknowable

—I mean,
think of it! Jesus
dying for a common blue butterfly
the one dotted with orange spots
a light indigo dusting
swerving into oncoming traffic
to avoid it.

How is it like that
that the dream keeps getting
more reality-like
and reality more
brochure-like?

At the crucial moment
a door banging open
in two sets of eyes
the dark pouring out
and the light streaming in

a violin solo raging
into the auditorium
of your soul!

—so incredible
I forget myself.

It's distinctly human
to look up.
Directly into the camera
at the supposed viewer—
yes, bloodshot,
haggard,
but beautiful, raw,

lived-in. A little sadder
and wiser.
And just beginning.

NOTHING IS EVER FINISHED ONLY ABANDONED

Always I am preparing the end.
The end is very old.

I keep arriving at it.
I sit in front of the camera
(stand-in for a third thing)

my hair brushed
my shine blunted, my teeth aching
to the point of madness, my body is taut;
one moment I am returned, then gone, then returned
to the day and city and time
the ground of April in a room—

Do you smell the scent of mud on the air?
Enchanting—this moment,
as if in time—Oh,

end! This is the sound of your voice.
And this is sound of mine.

PSYCHE

Psyche, you beauty; willow in the field, for you I shed my antlers,
I roll out my little jute rug to wipe my hoofs for you,
I take out my instruction booklet on how to assemble a bed,
but it is only theory. So I lay you down
in the nunnery of the pasture
until we grow moonlit, the gray bark and loam and light pronounced;
for chrysalis I spread a coat around our heads—

and when I wake,
I think someone is brushing my hair with a claw,
their smile hesitant in the continuum of joy—

it is only the objectless wind.

THE SHIP

In the discontinuous chair you realize
        nothing can wholly be written about or said.

You look up, smiling. It's almost laughable,

the beauty of dusk in summer,
the torment of nature! It just keeps going,

death flourishing,
        ruinousnessly becoming, it
keeps going. I tell you, it's
                laughable

to get high and look at it all,
            stepping into the other world
        you're already in, with your other face—saying of course

it is so good to live
        in the lucky fallout of words

said in a certain order in front of you and

        I still long—from my once
one-dimensional art

of impossible mourning—I long,
        a message, under the fold of an origami wing—

but I'd rather construct this giant boat, look at you,
and leave. My prow a naked girl

smiling under a white mask with red lips, in-looking, I plow
forward, the purple waves
        of the world fall together around me—

imagine it: to keep going.

        As if I had only one intention.
And it was to be

exactly who I am
        for the rest of my life.

LINE RECEIVED FROM AN INTIMATELY UNKNOWN SOURCE

Having ignored one light and given into another
I passed out of this life into the air.

Credits

"Old Bio In Snow," and "Rupture" first appeared in *Poetry*; "Theory" appeared in *Duck*; "What's Poetry Like?" Appeared in *The New Yorker*; "Students Singing Before the Flood" appeared in *Paperbark*; "The Temptation of Saint Anthony," "What is The Biological Function of Words," and "The Anxiety of Meaning," appeared in *The Glacier*; "Sprung From Nothing" "You Don't Know How Lips Burn, *Berlin Lit*; "Affuluence of Being," and "The Circuitous Path Towards Inertia," *Providence Magazine*; "On the Nature of Things," *Blush Lit*. Early versions of fragments of the following poems appeared in a chapbook from Foundlings Press, "Sound in a Dream," Black Sunflower," "Unsent Letter," "Dyad," Know Thy Other," The Color of What Fades," "You Don't Know How Lips Burn," "Sprung From Nothing," "Peele's *Nope*," and "All Ye Who Enter Here."

Ben Pease

BIANCA STONE is a Vermont-based poet and scholar currently serving as Vermont's poet laureate. Stone is the author of many books, including the poetry collection *What is Otherwise Infinite*, which received the 2022 Vermont Book Award. Her poetry and writings have appeared widely in such magazines as *The New Yorker*, *The Atlantic*, *Poets and Writers*, *The Nation*, and the *Best American Poetry* series. In 2013, she co-founded the poetry-based nonprofit Ruth Stone House, where she organizes events and retreats, teaches classes on poetry and poetic study, and hosts the *Ode & Psyche* podcast.